# Favourite Filipino Recipes

### Graham Woodward

# Favourite Filipino Recipes

Graham Woodward

Favourite Filipino Recipes

www.1889books

ISBN: 978-1-915045-12-6

*For Marietta – thank you*
*for all the help you have given*
*to me over the years*

# Table of Contents

Introduction   1
1. Filipino pork barbecue   3
2. Lapu-lapu escabeche   5
3. Chicken adobo   7
4. Beef pochero   9
5. Cebu style lechon manok   11
6. Beef kalderata   13
7. Humba baboy bisaya   15
8. Hamanado manok   17
9. Sour and savoury seafood sinigang   19
10. Filipino style BBQ spare ribs   21
11. Pancit Canton at bihon   23
12. Sinigang na baboy   25
13. Halang halang na manok   27
14. Traditional tasty and crispy Filipino lumpia (spring rolls)   29
15. Bantayan islanders lumpia   31
16. Torta mamon cebuano   33
17. Ube cupcakes   35
18. Filipino cheese cupcakes   37
19. Bibingka bisaya (bingka)   39
20. Cassava cake   41
21. Pan de sol (Cebu style bread rolls)   43
22. Turon banana lumpia   45
23. Leche flan   47
24. Coconut custard dessert   49
25. Ube ice cream   51
About the author   53

# INTRODUCTION

This collection of our favourite Filipino recipes existed before only in handwritten notebooks. Here we have brought them together for the first time in a book. Filipino cuisine is a combination of Filipino native based flavours with accents of Spanish, Chinese and American tastes. Whether it is stews, noodles, lumpia, or cupcakes and buns Filipino cuisine has evolved into something distinctive, and is one of the best kept secrets in the UK. Filipino Restaurants have not yet arrived in South Yorkshire! These simple recipes will be found useful to both Filipinos living and working in the UK for the NHS who would like a taste of home, or for people who just like to try Filipino cooking, there is something here to cater to your taste. I hope you enjoy them as much as we have in preparing and tasting them. We had a ball!

Graham & Marietta Woodward

## A NOTE ON INGREDIENTS

If you live in Sheffield the spices and herbs used in these recipes can be found on any supermarket shelves, but some of the more exotic ingredients such as gabi, okra, cane vinegar or tamarind mix can be found in international supermarkets – in Sheffield they can be found on the Asian, Caribbean and African stalls in the Moor Market.

*Back row: Banana Sauce, Cane Vinegar, Soy Sauce, Halaya Ube Jam Spread, Pure Sesame Oil, Sesame Oil, Fish Sauce, Oyster Sauce. Front Row: Salted Black Soybeans, Pandan Extract, Dried Banana Blossom, Ube Flavouring, Liver Spread*

Shrimp (crevette) cubes

Chayote (sayote)

Ube jam

Finger chillies

All purpose sauce

Gabi (eddoes)

Pancit (noodles): Bihon noodles are produced in the Philippines; they are the Filipino take on vermicelli (rice noodles), and either can be used. Canton noodles are the thicker egg noodles (like chow mein noodles) and are often used in stir fries and soups.

Ketjap manis is a fairly widely available sweet soy sauce.

Some tips about bananas: in the Philippines, bananas come in all sizes. The saba banana is a dwarf banana which grows mostly in the Visayas and has a creamy sweet flavour; they are used to make banana ketchup sauce. The large plantains which you mostly see on the British high street are imported from the Caribbean and Central America; they are okay to use in Filipino recipes.

## EQUIPMENT

Many of the recipes mention a dutch oven (an American English term for a heavy casserole dish that can be used on the stove top). Any heavy-based saucepan can be used in these recipes.

# 1. FILIPINO PORK BARBECUE

SERVES 4

PREP 60 MINS

COOK 25 MINS

## INGREDIENTS

900g shoulder pork
750ml 7UP
60ml soy sauce
100ml cane vinegar
2 tsp ground black
  pepper
1 tsp ground ginger
2 tsp paprika powder
250g brown sugar
6 cloves minced
  garlic
150ml oyster sauce
150ml banana sauce
2 tbsp sesame oil
2 minced birds-eye
  chillis

## METHOD

1. Cut the pork into uniform, bite-sized cubes to ensure even cooking, then rinse, drain and pat dry with a kitchen towel and place on one side.

2. In a large bowl combine the 7UP, soy sauce, cane vinegar, brown sugar, ground black pepper, ground ginger, paprika powder, the minced garlic, minced birds-eye chilli and half the oyster sauce.

3. Add the pork to the 7UP mixture and massage the meat, to fully work in the spices. Cover the bowl with cling film and marinate overnight in the refrigerator for best results, or 5-6 hours, before grilling.

4. In a separate dish combine the remaining oyster sauce, banana sauce and sesame oil and set aside.

5. Thread 3 or 4 pieces of pork onto each skewer, which should have been soaked in water for 30 minutes beforehand to prevent scorching.

6. Grill or barbecue the meat for 3 or 4 minutes on each side. When the meat starts to lose its pink, baste with the oyster/banana sauce mixture.

7. Continue to grill and baste turning the pork on its sides until the pork is thoroughly cooked through. Remove from the heat and serve.

TIPS – You will need 10 to 12 skewers for this. Before you begin cut the stalks off the chillies, slice open from top to bottom and scrape out the seeds with a spoon before mincing.

Very popular on the island of Cebu, this pork dish can be eaten and enjoyed on its own as a snack, or as a side dish with other dishes.

Cebu City has some of the best street food vendors in the Philippines and this is one of the dishes you will see on sale prepared on the stall.

# 2. LAPU-LAPU ESCABECHE

## SERVES 2

## PREP 60 MINS

## COOK 30 MINS

## INGREDIENTS

One whole sea bass
3 tbsp brown sugar
80ml cane vinegar
1½ tbsp cornstarch
½ green bell pepper
½ red bell pepper
Root ginger
1 red onion
3 cloves of garlic
2 tbsp rapeseed oil
1 carrot
1 tsp salt
1 tsp ground pepper
2 tbsp soy sauce

## METHOD

1. Clean the fish if the fishmonger has not cleaned it for you, and season with salt and pepper.

2. Deep fry fish, on one side at a time until golden brown and crispy and set aside.

3 Cut the bell peppers, ginger and carrot into strips, slice the onion and mince the garlic. Place in a wok and lightly sauté in the oil, being careful not to overcook, then set aside.

3. Dissolve the cornstarch in 3 tbsp of water, and pour into the wok with the cane vinegar, brown sugar, soy sauce and pepper and salt. Simmer for about 5 minutes or until the cornstarch has thickened the mixture.

4. Place the fish on a platter and pour over the sauce you just prepared.

5. Arrange the sautéed ginger, onion, carrot and peppers on top of the fish and serve with steamed white rice.

TIPS – Choose a plump, fleshy fish for this dish.

This is a wonderful dish: tangy fried fish with distinctive tastes of cane vinegar and bell peppers.

Fresh fish from the sea is sold in every Filipino market place, where there is a wide variety of choice. The fish traditionally used for this dish is grouper, or Lapu-Lapu as it is known on Mactan Island.

# 3. CHICKEN ADOBO

SERVES 3-4

PREP 60 MINS

COOK 60 MINS

## INGREDIENTS

6-8 pieces of chicken
  legs and thighs
3 bay leafs
5 tbsp soy sauce
5 tbsp cane vinegar
2 tbsp minced garlic
1 tsp cane sugar
4 tbsp peanut oil
2 tsp whole
  peppercorns
About 350ml water

## METHOD

1. Combine the chicken, soy sauce, cane vinegar, cane sugar and minced garlic in a large bowl, mix well and marinate the chicken for 4-6 hours, or better still overnight.

2. Heat a havy-based cooking pot and add the peanut oil. When the oil is hot, add the chicken and pan fry for 3 or 4 minutes on each side, or until the chicken is golden brown.

3. Pour in the remaining marinade and water, and bring to the boil.

4. Add the bay leaves and peppercorns and simmer for 40 minutes, or until the chicken gets tender, and most of the liquid is absorbed, then turn off the heat and serve with boiled rice.

TIPS – To make a pork adobo as an alternative dish, use 1-1½ kg of pork belly, or pork shoulder cut into 4 cm cubes and cook in the same manner using the same ingredients and technique.

Adobo sauce has a tangy flavour with a hint of soy sauce with pops of peppercorn heat which burst in the mouth.

This stew traditionally cooked in a clay pot over a charcoal fire is a staple cuisine in Filipino homes; it can be made with chicken or pork.

# 4. BEEF POCHERO

SERVES 3 - 4

PREP 60 MINS

COOK 60 MINS

## INGREDIENTS

800g braising steak
2 ripe plantain
   bananas
1 small carrot
1 medium sweet potato
2 cloves of garlic
1 medium onion
2 medium tomatoes
1 tbsp tomato paste
2 tbsp fish sauce
150g can of chickpeas
1 bunch of pak choi
Salt & pepper to taste
3 tbsp peanut oil
450ml beef broth

## METHOD

1. Cut the beef into chunks, place in a saucepan and cover with water. Bring to the boil and skim off any scum that rises to the top with a spoon. When you are satisfied all the scum has been removed, remove the meat with a slotted spoon to a bowl. Retain the beef broth.

2. In another bowl, place the plantain cut into 3 pieces; add the carrot and sweet potato, cut into quarters.

3. Slice the onion and garlic, quarter the tomatoes, and place in another bowl.

4. Remove the tail and any wtithered leaves of the pak choi. Break the leaves apart, rinse in cold water and set aside.

5. Place the braising steak in a clean saucepan, add the beef broth and bring to the boil. Season with salt and pepper, simmer for 1½ hours or until tender, then remove it from the broth with a slotted spoon.

6. Heat the oil in a deep pan (dutch oven) and fry the sweet potatoes, carrots and plantains until the edges are slightly browned, then transfer from the oil to a plate.

7. In the same oil sauté the garlic, onions and tomatoes until they soften.

8. Add the beef to the pan add the tomato paste; season with fish sauce and ground pepper.

9. Next, add back the fried sweet potatoes, carrots and plantains and add the chickpeas.

10. Pour in the broth from the saucepan and let it simmer to cook the potatoes and carrots and the broth turns into a thick gravy sauce.

11. Lastly add the pak choi and turn off the heat and cover the pan for 3 minutes to cook the pak choi.

12. Serve hot with boiled or steamed rice.

Beef Pochero is a sweet and sour Filipino stew made with sweet saba bananas that contrast with the sour tomatoes. This enticing dish brings out the Spanish influence.

Pochero is commonly served from a tureen in the centre of the dining table at family gatherings and celebrations, or weekend meal. Pochero is always on the menu in restaurants wherever you go in the Philippines.

As an alternative to Beef Pochero you can use pork belly sliced into bite-sized pieces, and make a pork broth instead to make a Pork Pochero. Taro or gabi can be used as an alternative to carrots; these are called eddoes in Caribbean grocers.

# 5. CEBU STYLE LECHON MANOK

SERVES 3-4

PREP 60 MINS

COOK 1h 45

## INGREDIENTS

1 whole chicken
1 medium onion
3 cloves of garlic
3 cm cube of peeled
  ginger
1 tsp ground black
  pepper
1 tsp salt
Juice of 2 lemons
3 tbsp soy sauce
3 tbsp fish sauce
3 stalks lemongrass
3 bay leaves
1 quartered plantain
  banana
3 tbsp brown cane
  sugar

## METHOD

1. Clean the chicken and dry it with paper towels. Rub the chicken inside and out with salt.

2. In a food processor place the chopped onion, garlic, cloves, chopped ginger root, sugar, ground pepper, lemon juice, soy sauce and fish sauce and blitz with 5 second bursts until a smooth paste forms, then remove from the food processor to a bowl.

3. Rub the chicken with the marinade you just made, inside and out. Place the chicken in a bowl with any remaining marinade and cover with cling film and let it marinate 3-4 hours in the fridge, or overnight for best results.

4. When you are ready to cook the chicken, remove from the fridge and let it come up to room temperature (about an hour).

5. Remove the chicken from the bowl and place on a rack in a roasting tin and reserve the remaining marinade for basting.

6. Stuff the cavity with the crushed lemongrass, bay leaves and quartered plantain bananas.

7. Preheat the oven to 190˚ C/375°F/ gas mark 5 and roast for an hour and 40 minutes in the centre of the oven until cooked.

8. Serve with boiled rice, (All Purpose) lechon sauce and a dipping sauce made in a bowl with 1 tbsp soy sauce, 1 tbsp cane vinegar, 1 tbsp sesame oil and 1 tbsp of chili sauce.

Whole chicken cooked and sold by every street corner vendor, Lechon Manok is very addictive to the Cebuano palette; it has a smoky, garlicky and lemony flavour.

Lechon Manok is traditionally a whole chicken rotisserie-roasted over a charcoal grill. It is a healthy and sumptuous meal.

Another lechon dish that epitomizes Filipino cooking at any special occasion or festival uses a roast suckling pig; the red-brown skin of which is considered the best part.

# 6. BEEF KALDERETA

SERVES 4

PREP 60 MINS

COOK 1h 10

## INGREDIENTS

800g cubed braising
  steak
1 tbsp minced garlic
1 chopped red onion
2 chopped tomatoes
1 tsp peppercorns
150g liver spread
2 beef stock cubes
250g finely chopped
  tomato (passata)
2 bay leaves
2 cubed medium
  potatoes
2 small sliced carrots
125g of pitted green
  olives
2 deseeded sliced red
  chillies
1 deseeded sliced green
  red bell pepper
1 deseeded sliced green
  bell pepper
1 litre of water

## METHOD

1. Cut the beef into cubes and place in a saucepan. Add enough water to cover the meat. Bring to the boil and skim off any scum that rises to the top with a spoon, simmer for 1 hour then remove the meat with a slotted spoon to a bowl.

2. In a dutch oven, heat a tbsp of rapeseed oil and sauté the garlic until fragrant. Then add onions and stir fry until soft.

3. Add the tomatoes and stir fry until they become soft and the oil turns to an orange colour.

4. Then add the braising steak and sauté for about four minutes, or until the steak turns brown.

5. Pour a litre of water into the dutch oven and add the peppercorns, bring to the boil and simmer over a medium heat for about 30 minutes.

6. Add the liver spread and beef cubes and mix until the spread is combined with the liquid. Then add the finely chopped tomato pulp (passata) and bay leaves and mix again to incorporate. Then cover with a lid and simmer for about 20 minutes more.

7. Meanwhile, sauté the potatoes and carrots, then add them, followed by the olives and chillies. Mix and cover and simmer for 10 minutes more.

8. Finally, add the bell peppers, cover and simmer for three minutes. Taste and add salt if necessary.

9. Serve hot with steamed or boiled rice.

TIPS – If you wish to make a pork kaldereta (kaldereta baboy) use belly pork and pork stock cubes.

This well loved dish is a mainstay in any Filipino household. A beef stew cooked in a tomato and liver spread sauce. Potato, bell peppers, pitted olives and carrots are added to the pot.

Beef Kaldereta is usually eaten at special events, but, believe me, there is no need to wait for a special occasion to enjoy this classic Filipino meal.

# 7. HUMBA BABOY BISAYA

SERVES 4

PREP 60 MINS

COOK 60 MINS

## INGREDIENTS

900g pork belly pork
4 tbsp cane vinegar
120 ml soy sauce
240ml pineapple juice
2 tbsp peanut oil
1 small red onion
2 tbsp minced garlic
1 tap peppercorns
2 bay leaves
2 star anise
3-4 tbsp black soy beans
Small can pineapple
 chunks
Pack of dried banana
 blossom
2 tbsp brown cane
 sugar

## METHOD

1. In a bowl, combine the 4cm cubed pork belly, cane vinegar, soy sauce and pineapple juice. Marinate in the refrigerator for 3-4 hours.

2. In a dutch oven over a medium heat, heat the oil and add a thinly sliced onion and garlic and cook, stirring occasionally until limp.

3. Drain the pork from the marinade and add the pork to the dutch oven and cook, stirring occasionally for about 20 minutes, or until you see the pork rendering and lightly browned.

4. Add the marinade which you reserved and bring to the boil without stirring for about 2-3 minutes.

5. Add the peppercorns, bay leaves and star anise, and stir to mix.

6. Add the black beans, pineapple chunks, banana blossoms and stir to combine.

7. Lower heat, cover and simmer gently until pork is tender. 20 minutes or more.

8. Add sugar and stir until dissolved. Season with salt to taste and continue to cook until liquid is reduced and pork is cooked.

9. Serve hot with boiled or steamed rice.

TIPS – If you are using canned banana blossom you will usually find 2 or 3 large pieces inside – these are not as pink as fresh blossom, but a bit greyish. Strip back the layers of skin, and remove the little tendrils of infant flowers and set aside and discard the thicker skins. Rinse the tendrils and remove as much water as you can. You might need two cans to make up the bulk.

This wondrous, warming pork dish has all the flavours of banana blossom, pineapple, star anise and salted black soybeans which impart a distinctive flavour, aroma and dark colour.

In pre-colonial days Chinese traders would dock along the seashore bringing their traditional cooking skills with them. This is one such pork dish with a Filipino twist.

# 8. HAMANADO MANOK

SERVES 4

PREP 30 MINS

COOK 45 MINS

## INGREDIENTS

1 kg chicken thighs
2 tbsp fish sauce
1 tbsp lemon juice
1 tsp ground black
   pepper
2 tbsp peanut oil
4 cloves of chopped
   garlic
1 small onion
   chopped
250ml pineapple juice
2 tbsp demerara sugar
2 tbsp soy sauce
400ml can pineapple
   chunks
Salt to taste

## METHOD

1. Skin and slash the chicken flesh with a sharp knife, then place in a large bowl with the fish sauce, lemon juice and pepper. Mix to combine. Cover the bowl with cling film and refrigerate for at least an hour. Then drain the chicken and discard the marinade.

2. Heat the oil in a dutch oven over a medium/high heat. Add the garlic and onions and sauté until the onions begin to soften.

3. Add the chicken and sauté until the flesh is no longer pink: about 5 to 10 minutes.

4. Add the pineapple juice, sugar and soy sauce and bring to the boil. Cover the pan and reduce the heat to simmer until the chicken is almost tender: about 20 minutes.

5. Add the pineapple chunks with the juice from the can and continue to simmer until the sauce has reduced and the chicken is tender: about 20 minutes. Season to taste with salt.

6. Serve with your favourite rice.

Hamanado Manok is another dish with a Spanish influence. It is a chicken stew cooked in pineapple juice and chunks, cane sugar and soy sauce often served at Christmas or on special occasions, fiestas and holidays.

Brighten up your Christmas with Hamanado Manok. Very simple to prepare and cook.

# 9. SOUR AND SAVOURY SEAFOOD SINIGANG

SERVES 4

PREP 60 MINS

COOK 30 MINS

## INGREDIENTS

1 litre seafood stock
1 lemongrass stalk,
   crushed
2 - 2½cm cubed ginger
   juice of 1 lemon
1 tsp granulated sugar
2 red onions, quartered
4 tomatoes, quartered
25g tamarind seasoning
450g fish fillets (such as
   cod or sea bass)
250g fine beans,
   trimmed or sliced okra
4 whole finger chillies
1 bunch spinach leaves
450g mixed shellfish
   (such as prawns, squid,
   mussels)
fish sauce to taste

## METHOD

1. Remove the spaghetti basket from a pasta pot and add a litre of seafood stock. Add the lemongrass, root ginger, lemon juice and sugar and bring to the boil over a medium heat.

2. Add the onions and tomatoes. Cover the pan, reduce the heat to low, and simmer for 5 minutes, or until the onions are soft and the tomatoes mushy. Stir in the tamarind seasoning (such as Mama Sita's or Knorr's Sinigang Sa Sampalok Mix) and stir to dissolve.

3. Next, put the fish in the basket, and dunk in the simmering stock. Cook for 3 to 5 minutes, until opaque throughout. Be careful not to overcook. Immediately share the fish between 4 soup bowls and set aside.

4. Repeat the process for the shellfish.

5. Now put the beans/okra in the basket and cook for about 5 minutes or until the vegetables are tender but still vibrant green. Distribute these between the bowls of fish and shellfish.

6. Repeat the process for chillies and spinach.

7. While the broth continues to simmer, taste and add fish sauce and more lemon juice if needed.

8. Remove the broth from the heat and using a ladle distribute evenly between the bowls with the seafood and vegetables.

9. Serve the sinigang piping hot with rice, or crusty rolls.

While many soups hit you with a restrained flavour, sinigang has an unmistakeable bold sour taste. This seafood soup is sour, salty slightly sweet, spicy and umami.

When I first came across this indigenous Filipino soup with seafood and vegetables and strong tamarind (sampalok) flavour, I fell in love with it.

# 10. FILIPINO STYLE BBQ PORK SPARE RIBS

SERVES 4

PREP 30 MINS

COOK 1h 10

## INGREDIENTS

1¼ kg pork spare ribs
3 medium red onions
2 litres water
2 pork stock cubes
8 tbsp soy sauce
¼ tsp ground white
   pepper
4 whole star anise
1 tbsp peanut oil
4 tsp minced ginger
4 tbsp honey
2 tbsp soft brown sugar
1 tbsp Worcestershire
   sauce
1 tsp sweet paprika
8 tbsp banana sauce

## METHOD

1. Place the ribs in a large stock pot with the water and bring to the boil. With a spoon, skim off any scum that rises to the top. Repeat until all the scum has been removed. Add the stock cubes and stir to dissolve.

2. Chop 2 of the onions into wedges and place these in the stock pot. Add 4 tbsp of the soy sauce, the pepper and the whole star anise. Bring to the boil, then reduce the heat to medium low, cover and let simmer until the ribs are tender when pierced: about 1¼ hours. Stir occasionally.

3. Meanwhile, finely chop the third onion. Heat the peanut oil in a frying pan and sauté the onion until soft and translucent, stirring often.

4. Transfer to a bowl and blend in the minced ginger, honey, sugar, Worcestershire sauce, sweet paprika, banana sauce, lemon juice and the 4 remaining tbsps of soy sauce. Stir until well blended.

5. Heat oven to 200 C/400°F/ gas mark 6 and line a baking tray with aluminium kitchen foil.

6. Using tongs remove the ribs from the stock pot and arrange in a single layer in your prepared baking tray. Brush over the ribs with the honey/banana mixture you made previously.

7. Bake in the oven, basting often with the honey/banana mixture on both sides, turning over with the tongs for about 30 minutes, or until the ribs are well glazed.

8. Serve with boiled or steamed rice.

These pork spare ribs are glazed with the sweet and tangy taste of the Philippines which comes from the honey and star anise.

These are super yummy Filipino Style barbequed pork spare ribs which are great at parties, or any celebration.

# 11. PANCIT CANTON AT BIHON

SERVES 4

PREP 30 MINS

COOK 1h 10

## INGREDIENTS

75g pancit bihon
150g pancit canton
500 ml water
2 shrimp (crevette) cubes
200g raw prawns
200g sliced pork shoulder
200g cooked and
   shredded chicken
Half chopped cabbage
1 medium carrot julienne
100g trimmed green beans
   or whole pois mangetout
Few sprigs chopped
   parsley
2 tbsp soy sauce
2 tbsp oyster sauce
1 medium onion sliced
3 garlic cloves, crushed
¼ tsp ground black
   pepper
¼ tsp salt
4 tbsp peanut oil
1 tbsp sesame oil

## METHOD

1. Soak the pancit bihon (vermicelli) in water for 10 minutes, then drain and set aside.

2. Dissolve the crevette cubes in the 500 ml of water to make stock.

3. Heat 2 tbsp of peanut oil in a cooking pot and pan fry the prawns for 1 minute on each side then remove from the pot and set aside. Discard the oil from the pot.

4 Add 1 or 2 tbsp of fresh peanut oil to a deep pan (dutch oven) and sauté the onions and garlic until the onions become translucent.

5. Add the sliced pork and continue to sauté until the pork turns light brown, then add the shredded chicken and sauté for 3 minutes more.

6. Add the stock, soy sauce and oyster sauce and bring to the boil. Cover with lid and cook for 20 minutes

7. Add the carrots, beans or pois mangetout and cabbage. Stir and cover and cook for 2 minutes more. You can add more stock or water if needed.

8. Add the pancit canton (egg-wheat noodles), cover the pot and allow the noodle to absorb the steam from the boiling liquid for about 3 minutes. Stir and mix the noodles with the other ingredients.

9. Now add the pancit bihon which you soaked and stir and mix until all the ingredients are well blended.

10. Add the pan fried prawns and season with pepper and salt to taste and stir and blend and cook until the liquid has been absorbed completely.

11. Transfer to a serving dish, drizzle with sesame oil and sprinkle with chopped parsley.

This is an amazing Filipino noodle dish composed of two types of noodle with a combination of mixed vegetables, pan fried prawns, chicken and pork.

This classic noodle dish can be eaten on any regular days, not just special occasions; it is a meal that will not disappoint. Try it with lemon wedges.

# 12. SINIGANG NA BABOY

SERVES 4

PREP 60 MINS

COOK 45 MINS

## INGREDIENTS

1 kg pork spare ribs
1 tbsp peanut oil
1 medium onion, sliced
3 cloves of garlic, sliced
3 x 4cm cubes ginger
3 plum tomatoes,
   quartered
1½ litres of water
2 pork stock cubes
25g tamarind soup mix
1 tbsp fish sauce
3 taro, quartered
150g trimmed fine
   beans
3 radish, sliced
10 pieces of okra, sliced
2 long green chillies
bunch of spinach leaves

## METHOD

1. Place the ribs in a large stock pot and cover with water and bring to the boil. Skim off any scum that rises to the top. Remove ribs and set aside.

2. In another large stock pot, heat the peanut oil over a medium heat. Stir in the onion and sauté until the onion has softened and turned translucent.

3. And the garlic, ginger and spare ribs, stirring occasionally until the pork has browned.

4. Add more water to that used to boil the ribs, to make it up to 1½ litres of stock, and strengthen with the stock cubes.

5. Add the tomatoes, fish sauce, tamarind soup mix (such as Mama Sita's or Knorr's Sinigang Sa Sampalok Mix). Stir to dissolve and bring to the boil, then reduce the heat and bring to the boil and cover with lid and simmer until the pork is tender and cooked through: about 30 minutes.

6. Add the peeled and quartered taro (also known as gabi, or eddoes) and simmer again for 5 – 8 minutes.

7. Add the trimmed beans and sliced radish and simmer for 3 minutes more.

8. Now, add the okra and long green chillies. At this point taste the soup if it's the sour taste you wanted. If it is not add a little more fish sauce or tamarind mix.

9. Toss in the spinach leaves, turn off the heat, and let the spinach finish cooking from the remaining heat in the pot.

10. Transfer the soup to a tureen and serve with boiled rice or crusty bread rolls.

Sinigang na Baboy is a simply delicious Filipino sour soup dish of tamarind broth combined with tender pork, vegetables, gabi and spinach.

One of the most popular of Filipino dishes it is one of those quintessential dishes you'll find in Filipino restaurants.

# 13. HALANG HALANG NA MANOK

SERVES 3-4

PREP 30 MIN

COOK 45 MIN

## INGREDIENTS

2 tbsp rapeseed oil
1 thumb ginger
1 medium red onion
3 cloves garlic
3 long green chillies
800g boneless chicken
   thighs
2 tbsp fish sauce
2 tbsp soy sauce
¼ tsp ground black pepper
2 bay leaves
1 lemongrass stalk
250ml water
2 sayote
400ml can coconut milk
2 red bird's eye chillies
Salt and pepper to taste
Bunch of mallinggay or
   spinach

## METHOD

1. Before you begin, slice the ginger into matchsticks, chop finely the red onion, finely slice the garlic, chop the green chillies, crush the lemongrass stalk, peel and slice the sayote and remove the stone.

2. In a pot, heat oil over a medium heat. Add ginger, onion garlic and green chillies. Saute until limp and aromatic, about 2 – 3 minutes.

3. Add the chicken, fish sauce, soy sauce, ground pepper, bay leaves and lemongrass. Stir to coat the chicken with oil. Cover with lid to let the juices from the chicken out. Cook for several minutes until the sides of the chicken are a bit browned.

4. Pour in the water and cook for 15 minutes.

5. Remove the lemongrass stalk; then add the sayote and mix.

6. Pour in the coconut milk and add the whole bird's eye chillies. Cover again and let it simmer over a low heat for 10 – 15 minutes until the sayote and chicken are tender. Add more water if needed.

7. Season with pepper and salt if needed; lastly add the mallinggay leaves or spinach and stir. Cook for another 2 minutes, then turn of the heat.

8. Transfer to tureen and serve with rice.

TIP – Deseed the green chillies before you begin if you do not like it too spicy, and if you like the sauce a lighter shade do not add the soy sauce (but personally I would use it).

Halang halang na manok, which simply means "spicy, spicy chicken," is a creamy and spicy dish with chicken, coconut milk, chillies and sayote (sometimes pronounced chayote).

Marietta and I shared this dish when we stopped over at a restaurant on our way to the Chocolate Hills on Bohol Island where it is a popular dish. It is believed to have originated from Mindanao in the southern Philippines.

Sayote can be bought from Afro-Caribbean, and Asian stalls in the Moor Market in Sheffield where they are sold as chow-chow.

# 14. TRADITIONAL TASTY AND CRISPY FILIPINO LUMPIA

SERVES 4

PREP 60 MINS

COOK 30 MINS

## INGREDIENTS

450g minced pork
2 tbsp peanut oil
200g raw chopped
   prawns
125g chopped onion
2 tsp minced garlic
2 tsp minced ginger
125g chopped spring
   onions
125g chopped carrot
2 tbsp soy sauce
1 tsp sesame oil
1 beaten egg
   pepper & salt
10 -12 spring roll
   wrappers
Rapeseed oil for frying

## METHOD

1. Chop the onion, spring onions, carrot and prawns, and set aside.

2. Heat a wok over a medium heat and add 2 tbsp of peanut oil and cook the pork, stirring frequently until you cannot see any pink, while breaking up the pork as fine as possible. Remove the pork from the oil and set aside to cool.

3. In the same wok, cook the onions until golden brown, then add the garlic and ginger and cook for another minute. Add the prawns, and continue frying until cooked through.

4. Add the spring onions, carrot, soy sauce, sesame oil, cooked minced pork and salt and pepper to taste. Cook while stirring until all is incorporated, then remove from the heat and allow it to cool.

5. When cooled, scoop out the mixture with a slotted spoon to a bowl leaving the oil in the wok as you do not want this in, or on, your wrappers.

6. In a separate bowl beat the egg and set aside.

7. On a clean flat surface lay out one spring roll wrapper in front of you in a diamond shape and spread 2-3 heaped tbsps of the filling in a line across the bottom third of the wrapper, then fold the two corners to the left and right, then fold the bottom corner over the filling and tuck in; roll to the top to form a cigar shape, keeping the lumpia as tight as possible. Brush the remaining top corner of the wrapper with beaten egg, then roll over to seal the wrapper closed. Repeat for the remaining filling.

8. Add the rapeseed oil to the wok to about 2½ cm deep and heat on a medium heat until the oil is hot.

9.      Place 2 or 3 lumpia in the oil and cook while flipping over occasionally until golden brown, then remove to a serving plate and serve with dipping sauce.

Lumpia are fried Filipino spring rolls, comparable to the familiar Chinese ones, and go by many names according to what is wrapped inside, which might include pork, chicken, prawns or bamboo shoots. This traditional recipe produces the crispiest lumpia ever. Serve as an appetiser or snack with a sweet and sour dipping sauce.

Lumpia can be paired up with fried or boiled rice or as an appetiser with a main meal such as barbequed spare ribs, or caldereta.

A dipping sauce in the Philippines is made in a bowl with 1 tbsp soy sauce, 1 tbsp cane vinegar, 1 tbsp sesame oil and 1 tbsp of chili sauce – stirred well to combine all the ingredients.

# 15. BANTAYAN ISLANDERS LUMPIA

SERVES 4

PREP 60 MINS

COOK 30 MINS

## INGREDIENTS

250g can of bamboo
    shoots
1 scrambled egg
200g raw prawns
150g cooked and
    shredded chicken
2 tsp minced garlic
2 tsp minced ginger
1 tbsp ketjap manis
2 shallots
2 spring onions
75ml vegetable stock
½ tsp white pepper
1 tsp salt
1 tsp fish sauce
10 -12 spring roll
    wrappers
Rapeseed oil for frying

## METHOD

1. Finely slice the bamboo shoots, shred the chicken breast, finely chop the shallots and spring onions and slice the prawns into small pieces and set aside.

2. Heat a tbsp of oil in a frying pan and make the scrambled egg and set aside.

3. Heat another 2 tbsp of oil and stir fry the shallots, garlic and ginger until fragrant. Add the spring onions and prawns and stir fry until the prawns are well cooked.

4. Add the chicken, bamboo shoots and scrambled egg and stir fry and mix together until combined.

5. Add the ketjap manis, fish sauce, pepper and salt, and a little brown cane sugar to taste if necessary.

6. Pour in the stock and continue to stir fry until all the ingredients are cooked; then remove from the heat and allow to cool.

7. When cooled, scoop out the mixture with a slotted spoon to a bowl, leaving the oil in the wok as you do not want this in, or on, your wrappers.

8. In a separate bowl beat the egg and set aside.

9. On a clean flat surface lay out one spring roll wrapper in front of you in a diamond shape and spread 2-3 heaped tbsp of the filling in a line across the bottom third of the wrapper, then fold the two corners to the left and right, then fold the bottom corner over the filling and tuck in; roll to the top to form a cigar shape, keeping the lumpia as tight as possible. Brush the remaining top corner of the wrapper with beaten egg, then roll over to seal the wrapper closed. Repeat for the remaining filling.

10. Add the rapeseed oil to the wok to about 2½ cm deep and heat on a medium heat until the oil is hot.

11. Place 2 or 3 lumpia in the oil and cook while flipping over occasionally until golden brown, then remove to a serving plate and serve with dipping sauce.

Bantayan Islanders Lumpia is a marriage of flavours between Chinese and Filipino cuisine. Filled with tender bamboo shoots, prawns and chicken it is hearty enough for a light meal or filling snack.

A dipping sauce for this dish can be made with 1 tbsp ketjap manis, 1 tbsp cane vinegar, 1 tbsp sesame oil and 1 tbsp of hot chili sauce, stirred well to combine all the ingredients.

Can also be paired up with another dish or served on a platter as a side dish on special occasions, fiestas and parties.

# 16. TORTA MAMON CEBUANO

SERVES 6

PREP 60 MINS

COOK 25 MINS

## INGREDIENTS

5 medium egg yolks
125 ml coconut water
1 star anise
275g self raising flour
1 tsp baking powder
60g unsalted butter,
  melted
65ml cold-pressed
Rapeseed oil
85ml condensed milk
110g caster sugar

## METHOD

1. Line a muffin tin with paper cases and set aside.
2. Preheat oven to 180 C/350°F/ gas mark 4.
3. Separate eggs, (you only need the yolks).
4. Make the syrup by heating the sugar with the palm wine in a small saucepan until the sugar has dissolved, then add the star anise and set aside.
5. In another small saucepan, melt the butter, and pour into a large mixing bowl and add the egg yolks; gently beat with a hand whisk to mix.
6. Now, remove the star anise from the syrup you previously made and add this to the egg yolk butter mix.
7. Stir in the rapeseed oil and condensed milk while continually mixing.
8. Measure the self-raising flour and baking powder and add to the mix 2 tbsp at a time while stirring until all the flour is added. Stir to fully incorporate so that you no longert see any white in the mix.
9. Scoop the batter evenly into the muffin cases and bake on the middle shelf for 20-25 minutes until a skewer inserted into the centre of the cupcakes comes out clean.

Torta Mamon Cebuano is a delicacy from southern Cebu. They are a sweet and spongy pastry, almost like a muffin traditionally made with *tubâ* and flavoured with star anise. They are eaten as a midday snack. *Tubâ* is made from the sap of coconut palm trees. It is a Filipino cottage industry. The farmer bleeds the coconut palm and collects the sap in a container which is placed below the cut where the tree bleeds. The sap is a milky colour and is poured into demijohns where it ferments from its natural sugars and yeast. It has a reddish tint to it because mango tree bark is added. When the fermenting stops it's ready to be drunk. The alcohol content is about 9 – 10 per cent. Unavailable in GB I found that plain coconut water works well which is available in any supermarket. Another alternative that works well is palm juice or "palm wine" which can be found in African-Caribbean shops.

It was the Spanish who introduced baking to the Philippines but it was only during the American occupation in the first half of the 20th century that milled cake flour was introduced.

# 17. UBE CUPCAKES

SERVES 6

PREP 60 MINS

COOK 25 MINS

## INGREDIENTS

For the cake:

2 large eggs
150g caster sugar
150m cold-pressed
   rapeseed oil
170g ube jam halaya
*1½ tsp ube extract*
225g self-raising flour
1 tsp baking powder
½ tsp salt

For the topping:

75g unsalted butter
150g icing sugar
75g coconut cream
A few drops of ube
   extract

## METHOD

1. Line a muffin tin with paper cases and set aside.
2. Preheat oven to 160 C/325°F/ gas mark 3.
3. In a large bowl, whisk the eggs, caster sugar and rapeseed oil until combined.
4. Add the ube jam halaya and whisk until you don't see any ube jam chunks remaining.
5. Add the ube extract and continue whisking until combined and the mixture is a smooth purple colour.
6. Measure the self-raising flour, baking powder and salt and stir in 2 tbsp at a time with a spatula from the bottom of the bowl until combined. Be careful not to overmix. If you no longer see streaks of white you're OK.
7. Scoop the batter into the prepared liners filling them evenly.
8. Bake on the middle shelf for 20-25 minutes or until a skewer inserted in the middle of a few comes out clean.
9. When baked, remove from the pan and cool on a rack completely before frosting.
10. In a medium bowl, cream the butter until light and creamy.
11. Alternate adding the sugar with the coconut cream, whisking until the mixture is light and fluffy. Add enough icing sugar to get the consistency you like. It should be stiff and not runny. Add a few drops of ube extract to get the purple colour you want, and mix to blend.
12. Frost your cooled cupcakes as desired, but be careful not to pile on too much of the frosting as this will overpower the cupcakes themselves.

Ube cupcakes are frosted little cakes packed with big ube flavour. Made with purple yam halaya jam, moist and fluffy they are frosted with ube coloured coconut cream.

Because an oven is not an essential appliance in most Filipino homes bread and cakes are sold in the numerous bakery shops in the Philippines.

Ube halaya is made from boiled and mashed purple yam and other ingredients to make a creamy, sweet and delicious jam and is used to flavour cupcakes, desserts and ice-cream.Halaya just means jelly from jalea in Spanish.

# 18. FILIPINO CHEESE CUPCAKES

**SERVES 6**

**PREP 60 MINS**

**COOK 25 MINS**

## INGREDIENTS

275g self-raising flour
1 tsp baking powder
¼ tsp salt
75g caster sugar
75g soft butter
2 large eggs
65ml rapeseed oil
100ml condensed milk
125g cheddar cheese
  (grated in 2 halves)

## METHOD

1. Line a muffin tin with paper cases and set aside.

2. In a medium bowl measure the flour, baking powder and salt.

3. In a separate bowl mix together the rapeseed oil and condensed milk.

4. Grate half the cheese and set aside.

5. Preheat the oven to 180 C/350°F/ gas mark 4

6. In a large mixing bowl cream the butter with the sugar until light in colour, then add the beaten eggs one at a time.

7. Alternately add the flour mixture and oil/milk mixture, ending with dry ingredients. Take care not to over-beat.

8. Gently stir into the batter the first half of the grated cheese.

9. Scoop the batter evenly into the cupcake cases.

10. Grate the second half of the cheese and evenly sprinkle over the tops of the cupcakes and bake on the middle shelf for 20-25 minutes until a skewer inserted into the centre comes out clean.

TIP – Freeze your cheese for a little bit so that you can easily grate or shred it.

Filipino Cheese Cupcakes are a must have at every child's birthday party. Cheesy, soft and savoury they are never frosted but topped with grated cheese.

Another favourite sold in bakery shops across the country, these are one of the best sellers.

# 19. BIBINGKA BISAYA (BINGKA)

**SERVES 6**

**PREP 60 MINS**

**COOK 45 MINS**

## INGREDIENTS

300g ground rice
180g light brown sugar
2 tsp baking powder
2 large eggs
2 - 400g cans of
  coconut milk
7g sachet of baker's
  yeast
1 tsp vanilla extract
1 tsp ground star
  anise, or essence
½ tsp salt
Parchment paper cut
  to fit muffin molds

## METHOD

1. In a large mixing bowl measure the ground white rice. Pour in 2 cans of coconut milk and give it a good stir. Add the yeast and give it another good stir. Now cover the bowl with a cloth to allow the rice to absorb some of the coconut milk. Move to a warm place and allow 2 hours for the yeast to work. By this time you should see bubbles form on top of the mixture and for it to have expanded.

2. Preheat the oven to 180 C/350°F/ gas mark 4 and line your baking tray moulds with parchment paper, cut to the right size, or paper cases. (In the Philippines you would use banana leaves.)

3. To the rice and coconut mixture, add the sugar, baking powder, and salt, and gently stir in to combine.

4. In a separate bowl, crack the eggs and add the vanilla extract and ground star anise or essence and whisk in lightly, to combine.

5. Now add the beaten egg mixture to the rice and coconut mixture, and stir well until combined.

6. Scoop the batter evenly into the prepared moulds and bake in the oven for 35-40 minutes, until the tops of the cakes are golden and a skewer inserted in the centre of the cakes comes out clean.

7.  Enjoy while warm with a mug of tableya, or chocolate drink.

Bibingka Bisaya is an exquisite rice cake from the central Philippines. Made with risen ground rice and coconut milk it is often wrapped in coconut leaves and served at parties.

Every family seems to have a different recipe for Bibingka which was traditionally cooked over a charcoal fire and still is in many homes.

You can use parchment cases you make yourself or can buy them ready made in any supermarket, or alternatively you could just use cupcake or muffin cases.

# 20. CASSAVA CAKE

SERVES 6-8

PREP 30 MINS

COOK 1h20

## INGREDIENTS

For the cake:

450g pack of grated
frozen cassava
250 g desiccated
coconut
250g condensed milk
250g evaporated milk
250ml coconut milk
5 tbsp caster sugar
2 beaten egg yolks

For the topping:

100g condensed milk
75g evaporated milk
100ml coconut milk
2 beaten egg yolks
1 tbsp plain flour

## METHOD

1. Remove frozen grated cassava from the freezer and allow to thaw out before cooking.

2. Grease a pan or baking dish with butter and set aside.

3. Preheat the oven to 180 C/350°F/ gas mark 4.

4. In a deep bowl, combine all the ingredients for the cake and mix well until the sugar has dissolved.

5. Pour the mixture into a greased pan or baking dish and bake in the oven for 50-55 minutes.

6. After the cake is baked, combine and mix all the ingredients for the topping in a bowl and mix well.

7. In a cup dissolve a tbsp of plain flour in 2 tbsp of milk and stir this into the topping mixture.

8. Pour the topping mixture over the top of the baked cassava cake and return to the hot oven and bake for a further 20-25 minutes, or until the topping turns golden brown.

9. Remove from the oven and allow to completely cool before cutting into slices and serving.

Cassava Cake is a Filipino dessert made from grated cassava. It is deliciously rich with a creamy custard topping. A perfect dessert for special occasions or an afternoon snack with a cup of tea.

Another dish traditionally cooked at home over charcoal but nowadays using a gas hob appliance which most Filipino homes have today.

# 21. PAN DE SOL (CEBU STYLE BREAD ROLLS)

SERVES 4

PREP 2h

BAKE 15 -17 MINS

## INGREDIENTS

200g plain flour
175g strong white
   bread flour
50g caster sugar
1 tsp salt
7g bakers' yeast
200ml lukewarm milk
30g unsalted butter
1 egg, beaten
25g breadcrumbs

## METHOD

1. In a large bowl mix together the flour, sugar, salt and yeast.

2. In a small saucepan, warm the milk and butter on a low heat until the butter has melted. Remove from heat and set aside.

3. Now, make a well in the flour mixture and pour in the lukewarm milk/butter mixture and a beaten egg, stirring to make soft dough.

4. Tip the dough out onto a lightly floured surface and knead until it becomes smooth and elastic. This should take between 5-10 minutes.

5. Form the dough into a ball and put it into a lightly oiled bowl and cover with a clean tea towel and leave it to rise in a warm place and double in size. This should take about an hour.

6. Tip the risen dough onto a lightly floured surface and punch down to knock out some of the air.

7. Knead the dough for a couple of minutes and divide into two even parts. Roll each into a log, then cut each log into 4 smaller pieces. Shape each piece into a ball and roll in breadcrumbs, completely covering all sides. Place the rolls on a baking tray lined with parchment paper about 2cm apart.

8. Cover with a clean tea towel and leave to prove in a warm place for about 30 minutes until risen again.

9. Preheat the oven to 190 C/370°F/ gas mark 5 and bake for 15-17 minutes or until the sides are a bit browned. Once done, remove from the oven and serve while warm.

As the name suggests of Spanish influence. Pan de sol are a slightly sweet, soft, airy and fluffy white bread roll with an amazing taste. Delicious with butter and jam or cheese, or eaten as a breakfast roll.

Sold from every bakery in the Philippines these delicious bread rolls are enjoyed hot!

A typical Filipino breakfast might include tapa: slices of beef or pork that have been marinated in a tasty sauce then dried, steamed rice, a cup of rich Spanish style hot chocolate, sometimes a fried egg and pan de sol.

# 22. TURON BANANA LUMPIA

SERVES 6

PREP 40 Min

COOK 25 MIN

## INGREDIENTS

8 small, ripe saba
   bananas
120g light brown sugar
16 spring roll wrappers
250ml rapeseed oil

## METHOD

1. Peel and cut the saba bananas in half long ways to make 16 pieces. (TIP – If using plantains cut in half across the fruit first. You will need four fruits), then roll the pieces in brown sugar.

2. On a clean flat surface lay out one spring roll wrapper in front of you. Place a cut banana diagonally across the corner of the wrapper, then fold the two corners to the left and right over the ends of the banana and then roll. Place a brush or your finger in a bowl of water and gently rub the water on the remaining corner of the wrapper. The water will help seal the wrapper over the banana. As you wrap each banana set aside.

4. Add the rapeseed oil to the wok to about 2½ cm deep and heat on a medium heat until the oil is hot.

5. Place 2 or 3 lumpia in the oil and cook while flipping over occasionally until golden brown, then remove with a slotted spoon from the oil and place on a paper towel to remove the excess oil. Repeat until all the lumpia are cooked. Transfer to serving plates and sprinkle a little golden brown sugar over the top of each one and serve with a dollop of ube ice cream.

TIP - saba bananas are the small bananas found in South-East Asia, they differ from the larger plantain bananas from Africa, the Caribbean and South America by being sweeter and creamier.

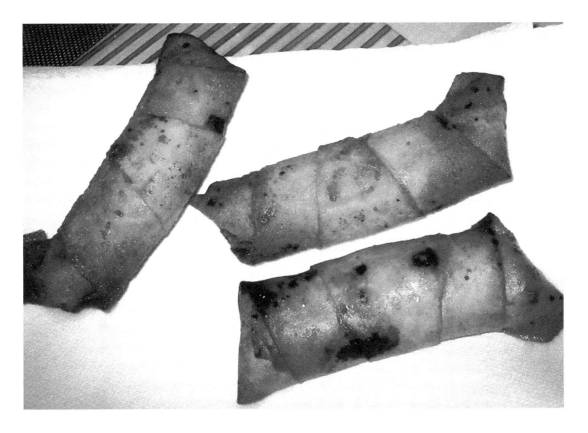

Turon are a common sweet, deep fried saba bananas wrapped in spring roll wrappers, rolled in sugar and served as a dessert. Easy to prepare for kids parties.

When I first visited my dark-eyed Filipina and family in their little rustic cottage in far off Cebu, I was served these delicacies by her mother straight from the wok.

# 23. LECHE FLAN

SERVES 2-3

PREP 30 MIN

COOK 45 MIN

## INGREDIENTS

60g granulated sugar
4 eggs
200g condensed milk
200g evaporated milk
1 tsp vanilla extract

## METHOD

1. Prepare 2-3 ramekins by greasing the inside of the dishes with a little butter.

2. Melt the sugar in a heavy saucepan over a medium heat and allow it to caramelize. Stir it frequently, since sugar can burn quickly.

3. When the sugar has liquefied and turned golden brown share the caramel between the ramekins before it goes hard. Tilt the dishes to coat the bottoms of the dishes evenly. Allow the dishes to stand for 10 minutes before adding the flan mixture.

4. In a mixing bowl stir the condensed milk and evaporated milk and stir until thoroughly combined. Beat the eggs into the mixture one at a time until the mixture is light, fluffy and creamy, add the vanilla extract and stir until all combined.

5. Share the mixture evenly between the ramekins.

6. Preheat oven to 160 C/325°F/ gas mark 3.

7. Make a bain marie: place the dishes in a baking tray and pour boiling water from the kettle, being careful not to get any water into the dishes. Make the water about 2cm deep or halfway up the sides of the ramekins.

8. Bake for about 35-40 minutes, or until the flans have just set, they should wobble slightly when you jiggle the pan. If they look watery give them more time.

9. After the flans are ready remove carefully from the oven and the bain marie and allow to cool, then run a sharp knife around the edge of the flan. Place a rimmed plate larger than the ramekin dish over the top of the ramekin and invert the flan on to the plate, so that the caramel is on the top. Repeat with every dish and serve with whipped cream, or ice cream.

Leche Flan is the Filipino version of Crème Caramel. It is a sweet dish traditionally served at parties, fiestas and other special occasions.

No party will be complete without Leche Flan being on the table, usually steamed they can also be cooked in the oven in a bain marie.

# 24. COCONUT CUSTARD DESSERT

SERVES 3-4

PREP 30 MIN

COOK 45 MIN

## INGREDIENTS

2 x 400ml cans coconut
   milk
3 eggs beaten
3 egg yolks beaten
160g caster sugar

## METHOD

1. Preheat the oven to 180 C/350°F/gas mark 4.
2. Place ramekins in a baking tin.
3. In a large bowl, lightly beat the eggs, yolks and sugar together until the sugar dissolves. Add the coconut milk and mix well.
4. Pour the mixture evenly into the ramekins and half fill the baking tin with boiling water to surround them.
5. Bake on the middle shelf in the oven for 35-40 minutes until they are lightly set.
6. Remove from the oven and tin and allow to cool slightly.
7. Serve with sliced mango, papaya or other exotic tropical fruit.

This is a rich and creamy coconut custard made from scratch using coconut milk. Eaten as a dessert, or served at parties.

An alternative to Leche Flan, these are also cooked in a bain marie.

# 25. UBE ICE CREAM

SERVES 6-8

PREP 30 MIN

FREEZE FOR 6h

## INGREDIENTS

300ml double cream
200g sweet condensed
milk
100g ube halaya jam
1½ tsp ube extract

## METHOD

1. Pour the cream into a large bowl and whisk until soft peaks form.
2. Carefully fold in the condensed milk and whisk again to soft peaks.
3. Add the ube halaya jam and extract, and gently whisk until all is combined and you have a blended purple cream.
4. Transfer to a lidded one litre container and freeze for 6 hours, or overnight, or until solidified.

TIPS – This makes a litre of no-churn ice-cream.

No Filipino can resist eating ube ice cream. Prepared from halaya purple ube jam which gives it its distinctive colour, it is often as an ingredient in making the dessert halo-halo (or haluhalo).

Filipinos round off their meal with fresh fruit. Halo-halo is uniquely Filipino and sometimes taken as a dessert, but often between meals as a treat. It is usualy served in a tall glass of crushed ice with a concoction of diced fruits (saba banana, papaya, mango, pineapple, jackfruit, coconut strips with pandan jelly), but also with things like red beans, chickpeas, gelatine, coconut milk and purple yam with a scoop of ube ice cream.

# About the author

Graham is a retired engineer and former project organiser (1989-2000) of The Ethel Trust Community Barge Project. He and his wife Marietta, who he met in Mandaue City in Cebu Province, Philippines, live in Sheffield, England.

## Also by the author:

Follow the author in search of his beautiful pen-pal in the tropical Philippines in 1989. Having found her in Rosita's, the store where she worked in Mandaue City, he is invited to spend his sojourn with her family in their rustic cottage in the compound where they lived. Sightseeing and trips to idyllic, deserted sugar-white beaches followed, as well as giving a helping hand in the daily chores.

Graham Woodward

I Married My Filipina Pen-Pal

The Girl in Rosita's Mandaue

with a foreword by Marietta

Working and playing together, they fall in love and decide to get married. Having found, and gaining, the legal requirements in Philippine and English law for a marriage to take place they are married in a civil ceremony in Cebu City.

Following their honeymoon on Bantayan Island, it is time for the dreaded British Embassy interview for a spouse's visa: that was denied.

The author returned to Sheffield without his new wife and launched a legal appeal, which was heard at the Immigration Appeals Court in Leeds a year later. This appeal was dismissed and a final appeal was made to the Immigration Appeal Tribunal on the Strand, opposite the Old Bailey in London, which overturned the previous ruling.

After being parted for two and a half years at the hands of the Home Office, they met again at Gatwick Airport, as soon as it was feasibly possible.

The book provides a colourful, true adventure with romance and passion in equal measure and heartbreak along the way with a twist in the tail.

CPSIA information can be obtained
at www.ICGtesting.com
Printed in the USA
BVHW021134281122
652926BV00019B/418